PRESIDENT TRUMP SELLS CALIFORNIA

DUKE Q. WALLACE

Parkhurst Brothers Publishers
MARION, MICHIGAN

www.parkhurstbrothers.com

Parkhurst Brothers books are distributed to the trade through the Chicago Distribution Center, and may be ordered through Ingram Book Company, Baker & Taylor, Follett Library Resources and other book industry wholesalers. To order from the Chicago Distribution Center, phone 800-621-2736 or fax to 800-621-8476. Copies of this and other Parkhurst Brothers Publishers titles are available to organizations and corporations for purchase in quantity by contacting Special Sales Department by emailing ted@parkhurstbrothers.com or by phoning numbers listed on our website. Manuscript submission guidelines for this publishing company are available at our website.

Printed in the United States of America

First Edition, 2016
2016 2017 2018 2019 2020 16 15 14 13 12 11 10 9 8 7 6 5 4 3 2 1

Library of Congress Cataloging in Publication Data: Consult Publisher's Website

BISAC Code: HUM006000 / topic / Political
ISBN: Trade Paperback 978-1-62491-080-7
ISBN: e-book 978-1-62491-081-4

Parkhurst Brothers Publishers believes
that the free and open exchange of ideas is essential for the maintenance of our freedoms. We support the First Amendment of the United States Constitution and encourage all citizens to study all sides of public policy questions, making up their own minds. Closed minds cost a society dearly.

Cover and interior design by Linda D Parkhurst, PhD
Proofread by Bill and Barbara Paddack
Cover and interior art by Bryant Arnold, www.cartoonaday.com

This is a work of satire. Those who take offense at this farce deserve a bag of cookies and a long recess.

01/2016

PRESIDENT TRUMP SELLS CALIFORNIA

"**BRAVO!** Now this is a book I can relate to! Wait 'til I tell my friends!"

—Art Buchwald, columnist and satirist

"**I** laughed 'til my sides split!"

—Jonathan Winters, writer and comedian

"**THIS** is my idea of public discourse. I highly recommend you read this book aloud to your loved ones. It's only flaw? It can't be sung!"

—Janis Joplin, singer-songwriter

This little book is dedicated to my mother,

Becky R. M. Wallace

who, God bless her, always
felt that her son might grow up to be president.
Were ours a perfect world, she would still be with us.

PREFACE

A NOTE BEFORE READING

Public discourse was once the sovereign domain of well-educated, reasonable men and women. No longer. Today, some of our would-be statesmen behave like circus clowns, vying amongst one another to act in a most uncivil and certainly unadult manner in order to secure coveted moments on camera. Apparently, they think we are all as vapid as those Roman citizens of old who could be enticed to vote for any whelp, provided they were given the day off, a hot roll, and a good show. I trust that you have a bit more sense in your head than all that. If you've purchased this book, then I must be right. Redemption is only nine chapters away.

1 GOD GIVETH AND PRESIDENT TRUMP FIRETH

THE CABINET ROOM, THE WHITE HOUSE, FEBRUARY 12, 2017

The White House staff had never seen the cabinet room in such uproar, at least not since President Lyndon Johnson arrived from Dallas on the same airplane that carried the late President Kennedy's coffin. Even the shooting of President Reagan at the Washington Hilton did not cause such mayhem in the executive mansion. Midway down the conference table, Vice President Palin was applying Sino-Qua-Non-Red lipstick prior to admittance of the TV cameras, radio network microphones, and—as she said when the doors were closed—"those Connecticut Pinkos from MSNBC." Secretary of State

Jindal was swatting away a makeup puff laden with Peach Lightening facial powder, which his staff beauty, Clarissa DeYoung, was attempting to apply. Miss DeYoung was only doing her job, and she did not appreciate the secretary's swat. Swats were okay on Sunday mornings when they lay about her Georgetown apartment eating cream cheese and salmon off each other's abdomen, *but not here in the Cabinet Room, for Crissakes! There is a time and a place for everything*, thought Clarissa.

With only eight minutes remaining before the media were to be admitted, presidential Chief of Staff Rush Limbaugh was very nearly pulling his hair out. Why had he allowed president-elect Trump to sweet-talk him away from his secure job at Broadcasting Prejudices, his radio gig of—how many years now? It must have been the offer of unlimited Viagra, thought Rush, his head swiveling automatically as if to be sure that nobody nearby was watching what he was thinking. *You have to admit*, he reasoned silently after confirming that everyone else in the room was fully engaged in concealing his or her own demons, *Viagra for life plus one hundred years was one helluva perquisite! The Democrats just didn't understand how President Trump knew his people,* thought Limbaugh. *That's why they didn't stand a chance against him!*

Seven minutes to show time!

The presidential Press Secretary, Ann Coulter, used her latest toy–a microphone connected to a speaker in the armrest of each chair around the Cabinet Room conference table. A word from her would shush the assembled cabinet members, senior White House staffers, and today's invited dignitaries. "In six minutes, I'll open the doors to the media," Miss Coulter announced in her most authoritative tenor. "The president will enter the room once all media are in place. As you have been reminded, his time is too valuable to sit idly by while journalists set up their TV cameras, deploy their microphones, open their laptops and arrange themselves in alphabetical order. He will join us at eleven minutes after the hour when his time will not be wasted by the antics of MMM (Trumpspeak for Mindless Media Minions). Once the president is seated, you will each make direct eye contact with him, in uniform expressions of executive adoration, as spelled out in your Pre-Fired Employee Manuals." There was a brief silence around the conference table, as secretaries of this and that let Miss Coulter's admonition sink in.

Now Miss Coulter's voice resumed at its highest tenor, "Serbs, open the doors to the media, please."

"Serbs?" asked Mr. Christie, the Secretary of Health and Human Services, without realizing that he had spoken aloud. The secretary decided that he had probably spent insufficient time reading his Pre-Fired Employee Manual, and settled back, grateful that nobody had responded to his silly question. *Live to fight another day*, thought the secretary of Health and Human Services. And he did mean *fight*.

At five minutes to the hour, the MMM doors opened to admit an onslaught of men and women wearing blue blazers, khaki slacks and skirts and carrying state-of-the-art recording equipment. Miss Coulter's lips formed into a perfect imitation of her high school drama teacher's arrogant smirk. Sure, He Who Fires (as President

Trump instructed her to address him) had required her to undergo a voice-change operation so that his press conferences would not be broadcast in what he had termed a "Mewing Female Falsetto," but this—THIS WAS HER MOMENT. For the next hour, she, Ann Coulter, former B-News talking head, was at the epicenter of power. Struggling to forget how He Who Fires had referred to that part of her anatomy (that epicenter of pleasure!) that the president so crassly threatened to have "cut out" if she failed to present him with the proper chorus of cabinet secretarial adoration, Miss Coulter remained as stiff as a North Dakota one-room-schoolhouse matron. She knew her Pre-Fired Employee Manual word-for-word, and she planned to be the last person in this administration to be fired. Miss Coulter figured she was good for three years, eleven months, and a day. By that time, she concluded while maintaining an eagle's sharp eye on the goings on between the MMMs and some cabinet secretaries, a consultancy at the think tank of her choice would be assured. Back to attention in the moment, Coulter knew He Who Fires would expect a full report following the cabinet meeting.

Three minutes to Trump Time! Miss Coulter addressed the assembled dignitaries, secretaries, staffers, and invited guests, in measured tenor tones. "Prepare yourselves for the entrance of President Grump ... er, Trump!" To Miss Coulter's right, Secretary of War W.A.R. Bombshell could not restrain a high-pitched titter. Miss Coulter took note of Ms. Bombshell's indignity, and at the way Secretary Christie locked eyes with the war secretary. Wanda Antoinette Religion Bombshell could be trouble. Miss Coulter could see that coming.

The majority-black high school band of Ferguson, Missouri, had been flown in to perform *Hair to the Chief* at this, President Trump's first televised cabinet meeting. I know what you are thinking, dear reader, but you are wrong. That was not a typo; He Who Fires had actually allowed a high school band to be flown in on Trump Duo (nobody but He Who Fires flew Trump Uno in this administration), and—incredible as it may sound—President Trump, a.k.a. He Who Fires, had actually allowed the band to perform a tune whose title might suggest inappropriate attitudes toward the commander in chief. Miss Coulter was beside herself when she had been informed by Chief of Staff Limbaugh just five hours previously.

"*Hadeees and Incantations!*" Yelled Limbaugh (whom Coulter secretly called "Limburger" when at home with her twin Irish Wolfhounds, Nagasaki and Hiroshima). "He Who Fires wants the American people to know that he is not above a little fun, even if it is directed at him, even if it is the work of a band of picki ... that is, Americans of Another Color."

Miss Coulter had almost lost her cool. Hell, she had almost lost her couture, which in this administration, she realized, would be tantamount to losing one's voice. Which–a moment later–she realized that she already had.

One minute to showtime!

The young musicians from Ferguson, Missouri, cut loose with *Hair to the Chief* just as He Who Fires strode into the room, followed by his Secret Service detail in their new,

Trump-decreed uniforms. The uniforms featured navy blue and white striped pantaloons, red vests and fezes, and white shirts adorned with silver stars.

Unable to contain her appreciation of the new uniforms, Secretary Bombshells elbowed the Secretary of Native Gaslands and Coalfields, Ted Cruz, and whispered, "Now that gives a whole new meaning to Secret Service!"

Cruz, whom He Who Fires had already chided as "Cruzin' for a Bruzin'" due to his irrepressible readings from scripture at the National Botanical Garden on Pennsylvania Avenue each morning at precisely 6:04 a.m., drawing what He Who Fires termed "undue attention from the MMMs," sighed grandly. The grand Cruz sigh was not in keeping with proscribed executive adoration, a note Ms. Coulter jotted on her tablet.

Disappointed that he was assigned the role of Cabinet Whip, with duties including enforcing appropriate executive adoration, the Canadian-born-to-American-parents secretary considered his future. Early as it was in the He Who Fires' administration, Cruz figured his long-term chances as secretary of Native Gaslands and Coalfields were only fair to middling. There would always be grand openings of gas fields in the national parks and ribbon-cuttings at new coalfields in the national forests. However, Secretary Cruz was unsure that he would not be upstaged at these occasions by He Who Fires (given the latter's manifest inclination to practice his Trumpishness at public events to date).

'When you got it, flaunt it!" Those were the words (of assurance?) that He Who Fires rattled off automatically when Secretary Cruz whined during a late-night visit on inauguration-eve. It was a moment of weakness, the secretary admitted to the president-elect, and not a very becoming one. He Who Fires had to agree.

Now that his first televised cabinet meeting was actually underway, He Who Fires knew in his white crew socks that he was in his element. It was kind of like the gig his chief of staff had before accepting the improbable offer of free Viagra for life plus a hundred years. *God, I'm good*, He Who Fires told himself, remembering *that* deal. *Barak*

Obama would'a never thought of that!

11 PRESIDENT TRUMP'S FIRST STATE OF THE UNION ADDRESS

CAPITOL HILL, WASHINGTON, D.C,

The House of Representatives Chamber was teeming with activity, as is usual prior to a president's entrance to deliver a first State of the Union Address. On both sides of the aisle, gentlemen and gentlewomen of both houses of Congress were busy glad-handing folks whom they would snub completely on any other day of the year. The television cameras were the reason for this seasonal cheer, and everybody in the room knew it.

The speaker's podium was unusually crowded this evening. Speaker Walkallover adjusted the lavaliere microphone that a CNN producer had attached to his lapel, next to the standard American flag pin and his *Make America White Male Again* pin, a special gift from He Who Fires on the occasion of the president's first State of the Union Address. Speaker Walkallover surveyed the room, making a mental note of those members of the House and Senate who have had the temerity to attend colleges and universities for a full four years. During his glorious tenure as governor of Wisconsin, Walkallover earned his Republican stripes by reducing funding to the University of Wisconsin by $250,000,000–an achievement which he felt received insufficient notice. *Overeducated policy wonks are the bane of my speakership,* Mr. Walkallover told himself, self-reassuringly, as he noted fellow members of Congress, who, like himself, made it to the Big House without the impediment of too much education.

To his right, the speaker observed Senator Toy Cottonmouth, the over-educated Arkansas fellow who couldn't stop at four years of college. *At least anyone who hears him speak grasps the futility of over-education,* thought the speaker, taking comfort in Senator Cottonmouth's eagerness to bomb the people of Iran, rather than take the time to talk to them first, as foolishly suggested by representatives and senators from the other side of the aisle. *Enemies of the State of Israel, every one,* thinks Speaker Walkallover, subconsciously patting the Italian leather wallet stuffed with cash donations from Those Who Think Right, the Israeli prime minister's Tuesday evening poker club in the basement of the Rayburn House Office Building. The wallet itself was a gift from the Israeli P.M. in gratitude for the speaker's last-minute change of heart on the Omnibus Overspending Bill, Department of War Edition, just last week. Embossed, as it was, with the Those Who Think Right logo—a bull dashing through a china shop—it was a token of immense pride to Speaker Walkallover. The wallet was one of the mementos he felt sure to find a place of honor in his personal museum now being planned for the vacated library space on the University of Wisconsin campus in Madison. *Serves those over-educated professors right,* thought the speaker, as he recalled with satisfaction the removal of the university's law library to a broom closet in the Chi Omega house.

Chi O! Chi O! It's off to bed we go! Walkallover just couldn't get that catchy tune out of his head after visiting the new library installation during his last month as governor. On that occasion, a cheerful rendition of the hymn had been performed in his honor by a chorus of busty sorority sisters. *It was such an appropriate conclusion to the library removal ceremony,* Walkallover reminisced, realizing that the chamber had quieted in anticipation of President Trump's entrance.

The blond shock of hair emerges! He Who Fires extended a hand, first to a member wearing a blue tie on the right side of the aisle, then to a member wearing a red tie on the other side. He was beaming—a grin so broad it reminded the speaker of that gecko who does stand-up ... or is it auto insurance commercials?

He Who Fires worked his way methodically, carefully, toward the podium. MMMs caught the twinkle in his eye as he seemed to be making notes about whom to fire, and when.

Now He Who Fires takes his place before the House, assessing the state of the TelePrompters. Through one, if he squints, he can see Republicans—yes! He smiles in approval! Turning, he squints again, seeing Democrats through the other—he smiles again! How remarkable, He Who Fires has smiled at the Blue Ties—on national TV! But wait, there is a sinister quality about that latter expression. Could he be planning a firing?

Speaker Walkallover, from his higher platform behind the president, glimpsed a quarter of the Adored Executive's facial expression, and Walkallover saw that sinister furrow in the presidential brow. So full of cheerful loathing was that expression. Might He Who Fires be ... thinking?! Oddly, inexplicably, it seemed to Speaker Walkallover—who had come to know the president so well, that He Who Fires *has actually reduced himself to the level of those college types. He was truly ... thinking!* It was a moment for the ages, and the clicking cameras, the bright TV lights had undoubtedly captured it for posterity.

Momentarily, Speaker Walkallover stood stunned. Then he remembered, and lifted his gavel with all the gravitas of that Jimmy Stewart movie—that silly farce!—and the great hall rang as the speaker let it fall, while he, too, was *thinking!*

Removing his baseball cap, the one emblazoned with his campaign slogan (Make America White Male Again), holding it aloft as if it were some made-in-China (which it is) crown (clearly, its hurried stitching declares that it is not). Finally, amid the tearful cheers, the president replaces it on his head and looks into the TelePrompter at his right.

He breaks down! Squinting past those words, Miss Coulter's words, Mr. Limbaugh's words, he reacts to the uniform executive adoration apparent in the eyes of the gathered members of his own party, the Red Ties. He hesitates ... can those be tears in the platinum eyes of He Who Fires? Yes, the president's eyes are misty. Can He Who Fires be overcome with joy? Or, is his expression borne on the light-hearted anticipation of firing eight or ten of those Tea Partiers who have already—in the first 35 days of his administration—become the pains in the executive posterior that Mr. Limbaugh warned him they would inevitably become?

Mr. Limbaugh's double-arm wave from the back of the room brings He Who Fires back to the present moment, and the president begins to read his address from the jerking TelePrompter. All is well in Limbaugh Land. (That's how Rush-of-the-Blue-Pills has come to think of this great land, "Limbaugh Land.") In his mind, he pulls the strings that make the country go. He, Rush Limbaugh of Cape Girardeau, Missouri, animates the executive who makes everything go. It is a thing of beauty in the mind of Mr. Limbaugh.

A grand, furrowed, king of pecans growing in a peanut shell.

The president's boyish enthusiasm is contagious: "Well, I've said it before and I'll say it again. America will not be safe for White Males again until we build the wall." Thunderous applause erupts from the Christian Coalition for White Males stalwarts among the audience. The president notices folded arms among Supreme Court justices, congressmen on the wrong side of the aisle, and many in the peanut galleries above. He resumes, "I have envisioned a wall 1,954.3 miles in length, one thousand feet in height, and twenty-one feet wide—with a foundation dug to the depth of eighty-nine feet below ground. It's height makes it unscalable, and no tunneling devices known to the Third World can bore under it." Thunderous applause from the Red Ties again, but this time not lasting as long. Miss Coulter is busy tabulating unsatisfactory responses, especially from cabinet members. W.A.R. Bombshell does the same as she watches the Joint Chiefs eye one another, their heads wagging discretely.

Coulter knows inappropriate behavior must be dealt with swiftly by those closest to He Who Fires. "Spare the wheat, spoil the chaff," that's what He Who Fires likes to say; Bombshell has heard it a thousand times.

"Turning to the home front," the president continues, noticing an uptick in executive adulation from White House staffers sitting behind the Supreme Court Justices, "We cannot afford to allow any Mexicans to be left behind in our neighborhoods and *boo-duh-warrs* once the wall is in place! *No Mexies Left Behind!*" The president shouts gleefully, apparently expecting another groundswell of applause. It does not materialize. Keenly aware of the underwhelming response to a line the president's speechwriters had highlighted as applause-worthy, Chief of Staff Limbaugh is beside himself.

Limbaugh is often beside himself when one of the pert White House interns from GWU leans forward in a scoop-neck blouse, but in this moment something different is happening. Mr. Limbaugh cannot smell the Limburger, so to speak. He is non-plussed, subtracted even. He is at a loss for context. *What? Don't these greasers get the president's profound meaning?* Limbaugh asks himself in thought. While most members of Congress are not truly greasers, Limbaugh realizes, the implication that many elected representatives cannot think any more clearly than your typical Birth Tourist seems deeply disturbing.

Limbaugh returns to the president's next phrase in progress, "... since we have defeated the Af'guns an' I'rax and brought stability and hope to the Israeli Region ...."

"Since what ... brought where?!" asked Vice President Palin, who could not remember having seen either the Slammic Republic of Irax or the Israeli Region from her front porch, back home in Alaska. She seemed to remember some dotted lines visible after ten p.m. while sipping from the case of women's lib likker Josephine "Dolly" Daniels sent up from Tennessee–or was it Alabama?–just last week. Such nice people, those Southern Likker lobbyists were, even if they had to go spoil her "only woman on the hot seat" party by convincing that left-wing California flower-maiden, Barbara Boxer, to run for another term in the Senate. *Aren't there enough women in the Senate?* The Veep had to wonder!

The president was pressing on. "During the first 19 days of our administration, the Amurican people have spent 17% more on contraceptive devices, jellies, and foams–a sure indication that those who call us a nation of immediate gratification couch-potatoes are surely wrong!"

The president waited for his logic to sink in. Limbaugh and Coulter had counseled against this thread in the speech, but He Who Fires had jovially over-ruled them. "I have my finger on the groinbeat of the Amurican People," he had said at the time. He never doubted himself. Neither his first wife nor his second wife nor his assorted wives' children had questioned his "finger on the groinbeat" thing, so He Who Fires figured it was good to remain in the address. *Some a-thuh intee-lect-shoo-ulls may doubt my instinct,* the president thought as he paused, *They may question my finger and where it gets its information, but I bet there are a whole lot of pickup-driving, dyed-in-the-wool Trump voters, who have their fingers on the same pulse spot as I do.* He Who Fires was pretty sure he had this groinbeat thing down. He figured history would remember him as perceptive, honest, and charmingly Politically Incorrect on this thing.

On this, Secretary of Health and Human Services Christie fully agreed with the president. Christie had never been laid low by the whole Political Correctness movement. *Movements are for the toilet,* the secretary thought as he eyed Justice Sotomayor out of the corner of his eye. *I've always had a thing for curly hair,* he mused, *and I can appreciate a woman with curves as much as the next guy.* Christie's smile and attention were not lost on the diminutive justice, who stifled a shudder, knowing full well that any shaking, however unintended, would only animate those very features that had caught Christie's attention. *They were not*, she knew, *her curls.*

After the speech, after the polite applause faded, the president stepped down from the podium, and approached the Joint Chiefs of Staff, reaching out to shake their hands gleefully. The president slapped each of the Chiefs on the back of his dress uniform. It was a bit of bombast that was endured but not accepted, if facial expressions were any indication. Then, the president lurched to his left to hug the new majority leader of the House. The majority leader, a former prosecutor, let his arms go limp at his sides to receive the presidential embrace. As his momma had instructed him on the first day of kindergarten,

Though kisses are wet
and hugs are nice,
beware of saliva and
avoid little lice.

Did the president notice that his embrace was unilateral? Not a bit; besides, he'd lived his life by his daddy's maxim, "It's not about the other guy."

Past the gauntlet of congressmen and senators, the president stepped into the bright lights of news media just outside the House chamber's big walnut doors. Grinning ear-to-ear, the president surveyed the assembled network, cable, and network cameras with real enthusiasm. The array of microphones encircling the lecturn almost glowed with bright alphabet-soup logos.

Taking a deep breath and adjusting his ball cap, He Who Fires approached the podium jauntily. Giving the speech had been great, but this, he knew, was his bread-and-butter opportunity. Act presidential, a little voice reminded him, and he took in a deep, satisfied breath before uttering a word.

The way his Secret Service detail moved among the media was personally gratifying to the president as he addressed reporters. Al Jazeera was present, he noticed, as was BBC World News—a realization that was better for the president's mood than the lithium he had taken before leaving the White House. A *natural high*, he thought as he pointed at a CBS correspondent, inviting the first question.

The reporter's countenance was deceptive–her face hovered serenely above a deep V-neckline, her lips glossed, and her ears lost in a halo of golden hair. *My type*, the president thought. But then the import of the reporter's query exploded like a rotten tomato upon the president's psyche. She was asking something about the administration's plans to annex Nova Scotia. "You have asserted, Mr. President, that the people of Nova Scotia share a common heritage with our own Scots-Irish immigrants, but how is that different from Mr. Putin's justification when he annexed the Crimea?"

The presidential brow furrowed of its own volition. The presidential scalp felt suddenly hot. "Clearly, Miss, ah, Miss, ah ... you have not read Secretary Dimmington's white paper on the merits of the annexation. Not only are our peoples inherently similar and ethnically harmonious, but Special Advisor Cheney has pointed out that the waters off Nova Scotia are home to the Western Hemisphere's most un-raped ... uh ... untapped oil reserves. Cheney has been manifestly clear on our destiny in the matter. Please, Miss ... ah, Miss ... Do your homework and that will clear up your question. I'll have the secretary send over a transcript of Special Advisor Halliburt ... uh, I mean, uh ... Cheney's testimony to the Senate Select Committee on Acquisitions first thing in the morning.

There were more questions and more references to Special Advisor Cheney, but everything was lost to the media after that. Networks, cable channels, newspapers, and bloggers had a field day with the president's failure to recall the name of a CBS correspondent who so closely resembled the president's second ex-wife. Commentators were unkind to the president in their analyses, but what galled him most was the gnawing certainty of his ex-wife's satisfaction at being compared to a hollow-cheeked twenty-something for a full news cycle, plus the weekly news roundups. It was too much.

III PRESIDENT TRUMP BUYS THE SUPREME COURT

ON THE STEPS IN FRONT OF THE SUPREME COURT BUILDING

The Supreme Court was asking for it, thought President Trump. *They have gone and done it.* The Supreme Court had affirmed the Vermont State Supreme Court and reversed the Appeals Court ruling, effectively ending oil exploration on the University of Vermont campus. Speaker Walkallover was standing before him in the Oval Office, fumes visibly rising from his coiffure. "Mr. President," Walkallover was screeching, "How in all that's Holy can the Supreme Court expect the people of Vermont to fund the University without revenues from the rich oil deposits that Special Advisor Cheney, has assured us lay beneath the campus? The only building that will be removed is the library, and Vermont can follow my example in Wisconsin by moving the library to a broom closet in the Chi Omega House!"

"Everybody knows that the Tri-Delts don't vote," replied a glum Cheney, apropos of nothing. Cheney sat, head in hands, in an overstuffed chair under the portrait of some president who didn't count because oil had not yet been discovered during his term. "We can't lose the oil and gas vote over this. If only the Supreme Court could be privatized," said Cheney, unaware that those free-associated words were about to have a profound effect upon the body politic.

"Privatized?" mumbled Press Secretary Coulter, apparently lost in a parallel cloud of thought.

"Just think of the possibilities for that Grecian palace they occupy," said Secretary Cruz, rising from the Kennedy rocking chair. Coulter looked his way, her golden locks catching the morning light from the window behind her.

Cruz, now standing, seemed lost in thought. "Just think of the theater possibilities, and the rooms ...."

Christie was cut off in mid-sentence by a revived president. Trump thrust an index finger into the air, and said, "I could run a court better than the Supremes. I think I'll buy it!"

"Buy the Supreme Court building?" asked a hopeful Christie.

"No, acquire the Supreme Court, the *entire* business," said Trump, his eyes rising to the chandelier as if to acknowledge the only other source of light in the room that could compete with his entrepreneurial brilliance. "It's basically a service business ... and it stinks! I could hire a turn-around specialist, a CEO would come cheap for that gig. Hell, Carly would probably jump at the chance. Of course, I'd have to allow her to spin off the Appeals Courts, provide her trademark surge to the bottom line."

Trump was clearly delighted at his stroke of genius. In his heart of hearts, he knew that even Cheney could not have come up with this one. "My people could triple productivity, cut out the fat, and utilize modern automation. Customer experience would soar. B.C. Rower and Associates will have to come up with a new award for the company that we'll form. You know ... Best Justice in Initial Quality or something. It will be big, I mean really *Big.*"

From the corner–if one can say that the oval office has a corner–a mumbling was heard from Chief of Staff Limbaugh. "Think of the licensing deals," he heard himself saying, before even he realized the possibilities. "Disney will be all over us for action figures, I can see a whole line of action figures. We'll call them "Legal Beagles," said Limbaugh, as if speaking from a trance.

"Don't get ahead of me here," President Trump warned. "My people know people in licensing. However, you are onto something. Write it up and I'll send it to my people."

"Mr. President," a feminine voice came from the opposite side of the room. "Wouldn't you have to change the Constitution to buy the Supreme Court?" It was that woman from Reading Is Fundamental, whose arrival for a long-standing appointment the president had overlooked. Carol? Her name was Carol something. "Wouldn't people think a president buying the whole Judicial Branch a bit untoward?"

Unaccustomed to being questioned, especially right in the middle of an entrepreneurial brainstorm, and more especially just as he was conceiving one of his best deals of the year, President Trump found himself chagrined, but something more than just chagrined. Speechless.

"Mightn't someone in Justice question the propriety of a sitting president acquiring the Judicial Branch as a private acquisition?" the woman from R.I.F. continued. The president knew about this woman. She had gone to church with Hillary back in Arkansas. That was probably where all of that over-education came from. Still, he knew she had friends on the Hill. *She might even have friends at Justice,* Trump thought. *She's been around here longer than I have.*

"Naw," said Trump finally, clearing the air–and his head. "Justice won't care a bit if I save the taxpayers from supporting all those old people who have kept their graduation robes for so many years after leaving college. Over-educated, every one of 'em anyway. Justice will look the other way if I replace the Supreme Court Library with an eighty-machine workout facility and give the Justice folks first dibs at noontime sauna access. I know those Justice types, they love saunas. They're crazy about them."

"And the sitting justices," asked Coulter, "how will we sell it to them ... I mean, their jobs are for life?"

"Golden parachutes for them," replied the president. "I understand your concern, what with that young woman, and all. But we'll give her a senior role in the new company ... or maybe she'll form some think tank for twenty-first-century justice or something. She's got CEO potential." The president seemed to be imagining Justice Sotomayor in a business suit, maybe something in a pinstripe, her curls cascading over her shoulders as in a TV shampoo commercial.

The woman from Reading Is Fundamental was not so sure, but her appointment time was up, so she demurely retired from the presidential presence, shaking her bowed head as she departed the West Wing.

IV PRESIDENT TRUMP FIRES THE ARMY

FORT LEONARD WOOD, MISSOURI

It is a fiercely hot summer day. The sun seems stationary, directly overhead. Everyone is sweating under dress uniforms as President Trump takes the stage. Flags stop moving as any semblance of breeze dies in the heat. Dignitaries on the dais include the governor of Missouri, the secretary of the Army, and Secretary of War Wanda Antoinette Religion Bombshell. Each one is squirming in the extreme heat, everyone but the man on whom all eyes focused, President Trump.

In his dark sports coat and grey slacks, the president seemed to be the only comfortable person in sight. His baseball cap, emblazoned with his slogan, "Make America

White Male Again," sat at a jaunty angle over his brow. He was a man on a mission, and it showed in the gleam of his eyes.

General Stuffedshirt stood to begin the introductions, which would include Congresswoman Staberback from nearby Jefferson City, the Governor, and finally Secretary Wanda Antoinette Religion Bombshell. It was a matter of formality, the president realized, but listening to all these underlings warm up the crowd–5,000 Army regulars and assorted brass–just seemed impertinent to Trump. He was ready to do his thing, raise some eyebrows, shake things up, and give the press corps the ratings bump they knew he had in him.

Finally! Secretary W. A. R. Bombshell concluded her introduction "of the man who needs no introduction" with the cheer Trump never tired of hearing, "Make America White Male Again!" Trump's mind wandered. Did the secretary ... *because in the modern world of today, you know, the medical profession can do things* .... Might Wanda, herself white but not a male, secretly wish that she personified the full Trump Cheer, or was she satisfied with her non-male status? *In this day and age, even a Secretary of War can have gender-upgrade surgeries*, the president reasoned. He realized he was smiling as he strode to the podium, a satisfied smile befitting the Leader of the Free World.

Adjusting the bill of his ball cap, the LOTFW grinned from ear to ear. The media is going to love this day, he realized. This will make their week. It will make their month. Hell, for those blondes at *Faux News*, it will probably make their year! Slowly following his gaze from left to right, the LOTFW knew he had these Army guys right where he wanted them: eye to eye, mano a mano. And he knew that he–the president of these United States–was Mano Number Uno.

As generals craned their necks for a closer view, anticipating his words–of what–praise?–the LOTFW lowered the boom: "Gentlemen, Women, Generals, etcetera, I am here today to announce a new era in American Military infrastructure, superstructure, divisions, subdivisions, companies, and freelancers! I am here to share with you the results of my thinking on the security of our country and the place of our Army."

Every eye was riveted on the LOTFW and he loved it. It was another signature Trump moment. Chief of Staff Limbaugh was beaming, Press Secretary Coulter was beaming. *Sure*, the president thought, *they know what's coming. I'm a genius, a damned genius whose time has come! This is big, really big! The people are going to be crazy for this. Just Crazy!*

Then he spelled it out. "The place of the Army in our current multiple war plan? There is no place. The Army is an institution whose time has come ... and gone! The Army is so fifteen minutes ago."

Into the silence, the absolute hear-a-paperclip-drop silence that followed, the LOTFW continued, his smile unbroken. "The Army was great back in WW2. The Army had guys like Patton, actually one Patton, but lots of good guys. They made war the way I fire people, with real guts. But today's Army just doesn't get good ratings. All those videos from Abu Ghraib ... disgusting! And those persistent reports of $3,000 wrenches ... Insufferable! But back to that whole team thing ... Altogether fifteen minutes ago! Can't even keep its own in line. Bombing a hospital in Afghan-iss-tan, deplorable. Just not a ship-shape outfit anymore.

"I'll tell you what Amurica needs, and I'm going to see that Amurica gets what it needs. We need a fighting force that kicks butt. Not some pansies who come home after failing to make the deal and then commit suicide. What's with that? Army guys have forgotten which is the business end of their Colt 45s? Or whatever."

"I liked those commercials that proclaimed 'an army of one.' I'm one; I could understand that. But now your commercials ask red-blooded Amurican men to be part of a teeeeam! Teams are for tennis, not for killing. Only a man can kill a man! What's with all this teeeeam shit?!

"You guys go home. Go back to your momma and cuddle up in her rocking chair. You're a bunch of pussies. No better than a bunch of groundhogs–I mean the little, furry, four-legged kind. Go home. You're fired."

Heads turned. Hell, heads rolled! Guys who had been standing at attention for the duration of the ceremony so far began to slump, to lower their rifles to the sand, to chatter amongst themselves. What he serious? Am I fired? Where will my next paycheck come from? Questions were flying.

On the dais, Secretary of War Bombshell was now standing beside the LOTFW, asking herself whether she should intervene, because the president's words were news to her, just as they were to the assembled Army recruits, regulars, and brass. She knew she was tough, but Secretary Bombshell was as blindsided by the president's words as the live TV audience. Watching the president's speech on CNN, CBS, ABC, and Faux News, tens of millions sat back and looked at one another in wonder.

President Trump turned to face the secretary of war. The president was calm. He had made a decision and announced it. Wasn't that the way the world worked? Why had Secretary W.A.R. Bombshell left her chair and approached the microphone while he was speaking? The LOTFW thought the secretary was out of order. He was ready to proceed. He was prepared to tell the nation how he planned to replace the Army with a more efficient force, a better killing machine. Twisting his ball cap as if to remind the secretary (and the thousands of soldiers, who were now breaking ranks and wandering about aimlessly) how the F-35 ate the cabbage.

But, to use Press Secretary Coulter's learned phraseology, the Holstein was out of the House. That was apparent. A president can speak, but even the LOTFW needs an audience, and President Trump had just lost his. It would be inappropriate for him to continue to speak to such a boisterous crowd. It just wouldn't be Trumply.

That much was clear. So the LOTFW beat a strategic retreat back to Trump Uno, which was gassed up and ready to move on.

Let these losers go home to momma and lick their wounds, Trump thought as he returned to his presidential motorcade and it sped off toward the airport. *That's what losers do. Always has been, always will be.*

The news media was in full crisis mode. Near the dais, talking heads were hastily rethinking their planned commentaries. Correspondents stood in front of cameras ... dazed and mute. All the analyses that had been painstakingly prepared prior to the president's arrival had to be thrown out. On site, camera crews turned from dumbstruck reporters to focus on thousands of uniformed soldiers who had just been fired. As the enlisted men wandered about, milling back and forth with no apparent direction, TV producers in nearby production vans scrambled to fill dead time with canned patriotic music. Back in New York, managing editors of newspaper syndicates were assembling editorial teams to cover various aspects of the story.

At the New York Times on Eighth Avenue, all of the Bigwigs and many of the Lesserwigs were huddled in a conference room where the latest bombshell from President Trump lay like an unexploded missile as long as the conference table.

"Anybody got a line on this?" asked the editor-in-chief.

"What's the angle?" asked an assistant to the publisher.

Someone who's title was unclear blurted, "What's the LOTFW got under that baseball cap now?" It was the question of the moment, of the hour, of the whole damned first one hundred days. There was no immediate response. Seasoned newsmen and women knew that stepping into a Trump-made quagmire like this one could cost somebody a sterling four-decade reputation faster than you can say, "LOTFW."

Trump Uno was approaching home base, Andrews Air Force Base outside Washington, D.C. The LOTFW was grinning that trademark grin. Pleased with his performance, the president was surfing the web, checking to see if new polling numbers had been uploaded since his speech in Missouri. *It was a Heartland performance*, he complimented himself enthusiastically, *a Heartland perfor-*

mance worthy of William Jennings Bryan, Teddy Kennedy, Bob Freakin' Dole, and Senator Al Franken combined!

The LOTFW enjoyed stirring things up in a big way. *I'm a P.T. Barnum kinda guy*, he congratulated himself again. *Hell, even a Kennedy couldn't have pulled that off!* In his heart of hearts, Trump knew that he was right, The Army was outdated, outmoded, and bloated. The recent Army television commercials showed it for all to see. The Marine Corps outclassed them in every way, from the shiny brass buttons on those amazing blue dress uniforms to the snappy white slacks and matching dress hats. The Marine Corps looks like a Number One outfit, and the ratings of their TV commercials were the proof of it, broadcast for all the world to see.

Besides, the Marine Corps commandant had the class to enter the highest bid. Hell, the commandant started the whole bidding process. It was his idea, and the president liked it a lot. When the Army got a whiff of it, it was just too damned late. A pound short and a penny late, that Army general had the gall to act offended by the idea of bidding to become the country's only infantry outfit. Where did he get the idea that, once an Army always an Army? Just absolutely fifteen minutes ago!

Tomorrow, the president told himself, *tomorrow I will announce the savings to our budget made possible by firing the* Army. *I'll do it from the Rose Garden. Get it*, he thought, *reveling in the irony of it, roses go with firing the Army! Jerry Garcia would love it! It's too perfect!*

V PRESIDENT TRUMP REDRESSES CONGRESS

KENNEDY CENTER FOR THE PERFORMING ARTS, WASHINGTON, D.C.

It was the first Saturday in May, and the Japanese Cherry trees around Washington, D.C., were in full bloom. The president's wife and daughters were busy busting champagne bottles on a new nuclear submarine up in New London, Connecticut.

President Trump spent the day golfing at Camp Trump (formerly Camp David) with his sons, looking forward to the evening's festivities at the Kennedy Center for the Performing Arts. *Gotta remember to rename that place,* Trump made a mental note as he sliced magnificently on the eighth hole. *"Kennedy" is such a passe' name, makes our democracy look so inept, so fifteen minutes ago.* Congratulating himself for his forward thinking as he high-stepped through the rough in search of his ball, the LOTFW realized he would need to change shoes before his end-of-round press conference. *Can't have scratched shoes when I give the cameras a teaser about tonight's big announcement,* President Trump thought.

The late afternoon press conference was just a warm-up for the president. His only intent was to alert the media to give special focus to his evening at the Kennedy Center. Sure, they would attend, but he wanted to make it clear to them from the outset that this would not be just another evening of socializing with the artist- and composer-types. His thinly-veiled line about "seeing that our senators and congressmen–and women–are properly suited for the work ahead" was so subtle, by Trump standards, that it went right over the heads of most of the press corps. "Just one more way this president is plunging his fingers into the blackbird pie," reported one of the Faux blondes.

When President Trump heard that coverage, he spat back

at the screen: "Darlin', just you keep your little self on the sidelines while I show you what a real man can do!" The blonde had a lesson coming, Trump could see plain as day. And he was just the man to administer it.

On Marine Corps One, the formerly green-and-white helicopter used to ferry commanders-in-chief around Washington, D.C., the LOTFW confided in his portly chief legislative aide. "When I unveil my plan to redress Congress, you can bet my polling numbers will hit a new high. The gays, lesbos and their like are gonna love what I've been able to do with a few hundred thousand yards of Rayon. Shoot, we are gonna need fourteen yards just to cover you!" Pleased with his spontaneous humor, the president missed the chief legislative aide's scowl, but the LOTFW recalled how satisfying it was to "pinch an inch" of his aide's gut. *Pinch an inch, my ass*, thought the president. *Grab some flab is more like it.* The president filed that line away for use when he eventually met Kim Jung Un, who was looking more portly each time he appeared on TV news.

When the presidential motorcade arrived at the secure entrance to the Kennedy Center, President Trump was in the best of moods. He was on top of his game, and he knew it. The Army brass had taken their firing–and that of their 895,648 regulars and 839,753 reservists–like gentlemen (and women). Sure, the golden parachutes extended to all 386 general officers had helped, but all told, they'd hardly received more than Carly Fiorina had banked after leaving HP. *Okay, so throw in the golden parachutes of three or four bank CEOs, and the scales are balanced. A drop in the bucket*, the LOTFW figured. A pittance, in the grand scheme of things.

The Marines will get all of those Army tanks repainted in Corps colors before the month is out. Then our bases will look more like winning centers, instead of losing centers. The color is symbolic. Properly used, color is a transformational tool, a motivational magnet!

At the podium forty-five minutes later, the LOTFW appeared relaxed, confident, and ready to give the media another of his trademark rating bumps. It's a role he enjoyed, something unique that only he could pull off. "Don't call it hubris," one news analysis had said recently, "because it really is this president's special gift. Give him a microphone and he can draw the ratings." Nobody could deny it.

"Let's face it," the president opened, twisting his torso as he mauled the podium before the packed house, "It is time to redress the Congress. I'm sure that my people are not the only ones who have gotten tired of the whole red tie/blue tie thing. Red ties for my party. Blue ties for my former party. Ties and states: red, blue .... Dull. Dull. *Dull,*" the president said, emphasizing the final syllable with a rising voice and a meaty hand-slam on the podium.

"The time has come to stop with the wishy-washy red and blue ties. Since I've officed on Fifth Avenue for twenty years or so, through thick and thin, I've become an astute arbiter of fashion. So let me tell you how Donna Karan ate the cabbage ...." The president was particularly pleased with this turn of phrase. Besides, cabbage was his grand-mother's favorite vegetable. She extolled the versatility of cabbage many a day. Cole slaw. Sauerkraut. Bean soup with cabbage. Not to mention cabbage rolls. Versatile. And cheap. Those Mexicans who farm Southern California could grow cabbages by the billions, trillions maybe.

"In a minute here, we are going to unveil the new dress uniform for members of Congress. There is nothing to fear, nothing so fancy as my Secret Service detail wears. My boys–and girls–are in a league of their own. I came up with a look that won't shock visiting dignitaries or embarrass anyone. You in the Congress–even senators–can keep your white shirts. I'm okay with that." The president seemed to sense that the audience needed a minute to take in the grandeur of his coming announcement, and he was prepared for that. Secretary of Native Gaslands and Coalfields Cruz was standing in the wings ready to read *Green Mayo and Spam*, that classic picture book written by that medical doctor from Patterson, New Jersey. That guy musta been ADHD–being an M.D. wasn't enough to occupy his mind! Surely that would calm the audience in the cavernous hall. By the time Secretary Cruz had read *Green Mayo and Spam* thirteen times, attendees and honorees alike were feeling decidedly recumbent, even somnolent.

That was President Trump's cue to continue with the evening program proper, and goodness knows he was itching to get the show on the road. "Behind Door Number One, we have the member of Congress from my party wearing ...." All eyes in the audience were focused on Door Number One, which now rolled up to reveal a middle-aged Congressman from the third district of Virginia wearing a suit of fashionable cut ... tailored out of the reddest of fire engine red sharkskin fabric. The congressman was red from his neck down to his white crew socks. His shirt was white, sure enough, and his tie was a tasteful gray, but his suit coat and slacks were as red as red could be. "Nobody will mistake anyone dressed like this for an auto executive or for the commissioner of baseball," said the president, an understatement which no person in the vast theater could dispute.

Next, the president saluted Door Number Two, from which emerged a senator, the Junior Senator from the

Great State of Michigan. The senator stepped forward into the bright set lights and made a valiant half-smile. His shirt was as white as any you've seen on the evening news. His tie was an elegant silver. His suit coat and slacks, however, were the bluest of blues. Not a subtle navy blue, not a demure light blue, but a shocking blue that sent spines digging into seat backs throughout the theater. Somehow, President Trump's people had found a blue so magnified in intensity that viewing it—just glancing at it—was painful to the eyes.

As the models—perhaps fifty of them, in attire that alternated from shocking red to blinding blue—coursed along a runway that had unexpectedly appeared, a kind of dark mechanical tongue that extended itself out above the first eight or ten rows of the audience, audible gasps arose from those seated nearest. The procession of red suits and blue suits seemed as gear-driven as the extension of the runway itself—as if the redressed Congress had instantly been transformed into an Orwellian parade of automatons.

VI President Trump Nationalizes the Girl Scouts

A Strange Phone Call Is Received at Cookie Drive Headquarters, USA

Operator: "Cookie Drive Headquarters; how may I help you today?

Unidentified Caller: "Is this the Cookie Drive Operations Center? The Situation Room? The Office of the CEO?"

O: "Well, sir, this is the office from whence all cookies are driven. We like to call it, 'the SUV Vortex, Station Wagon Central, Minivan Heaven.' What is it that we can do for you here at the Heavenly Vortex?"

UC: "I was hoping to speak with the Supreme Cookie

Driver!"

O: "Oh, sir, I just know we can satisfy your sweet tooth today! Our girls are prepared to knock on thirty-seven million doors and set up shop in front of three point eight million big box stores to serve you wherever you may ...."

UC: "Just put the CEO on the line, dear. Save the statistics for my people."

O: "There is a small problem with that, sir. Our 'Supreme Cookie Driver,' as you put it, has just lifted off aboard Green Dress Number One, bound for Seattle."

UC: "Seattle? What's in Seattle? O: "I'm afraid I can't disclose Girl Scout Ops, sir. Her mission is top secret, strictly hush-hush."

UC: "Sounds like the kind of gal I need for the job I have in mind."

O: "Sir! Please do not even think of raiding our Corporate Sweet ... er, Suite! We would be lost without her!"

UC: "Aw, take a Valium, miss! I don't want one person,

sister; I want the whole she-bang. Just connect me with your CEO."

O: "Since Cookie Fairy Supreme is away, sir, may I transfer you to Cookie Creations Laboratories? Sir? It sounds as if you may have a new product concept to discuss with our people in Cookie Creations ...."

UC: "I've discussed conception with a woman or two in my time, you bet I have. It's been said that my conception discussion skills are second to none. Why, once, I spent all night discussing conception with the Princess of ...."

O: "Excuse you, sir; your line of ... well, your line seems to have wandered ...."

Click.

[Twenty-three minutes later]

O: "Cookie Drive Headquarters; how may I help you today?"

Familiar Voice: "Yes, ah ... May I speak to the Boss Lady,

please?"

O: "I will be happy to connect you to her office, sir. Whom may I say is calling?"

FV: "Oh, I think she will know my voice when she hears it."

O: "Now, sir, I know this isn't the voice of Mr. Supreme Cookie Consort; I know his ...."

FV: "Enough with the pleasantries, sister. Put the Boss Lady on the line!"

O: "I will transfer you to her executive assistant, sir, but I advise...."

FV: "Enough of your help, sister! Just put 'er on!"

Recorded Voice: "Our on-hold music has been provided by Girl Scout Troop 59 of Tulsa, Oklahoma ..." [to the tune of *It's a Small World*]

It's a green, green world,
full of sugar and spice,
frosted cherry or chocolate

topping gluten or rice ...
It's a green, green world ....

Executive Assistant: "Good morning; Office of the Supreme Cookie Goddess. Who may I say is calling?"

Unidentified Caller: "I am calling, you over-educated, Oxford-dialect-in-a-pantsuit! Just put the Boss Lady on the line or you'll be fired!"

EA: "Sir! I assure you that kind of verbal abuse will get you nowhere! You ..."

UC: "Look, girlie, that kind of talk has made me the deal-maker of the decade, the billionest-billionaire of the business world, and now the god-damned presi ..."

EA: "Hyperbole will get you nowhere, I assure ..."

UC: "Give me any more gruff, girlie, and I'll put my pole to your hy ..."

EA: "Sir! You are out of line, sir ...."

UC: "You don't know the half, the third, the quarter of

it, sister ....”

Click.

The executive assistant to the Supreme Cookie Goddess had never hung up on anyone before. Asking herself whether she had just cost the Girl Scouts the deal of the decade, she answered in the negative. Surely, she reasoned, anyone so uncouth could not have risen sufficiently high in the world as to amass even a personal 401(k), let alone enough of a fortune to benefit the Girl Scouts of America.

[Meanwhile aboard Green Dress Number One, flying at 33,000 feet above the Continental Divide, the satellite phone of the Supreme Cookie Goddess, which has never before rung during flight, rings.]

Surprised Cookie Goddess: “... Harvey? I’ve told you not to use this line. It costs the Girl Scouts eighteen dollars per minute and is only for emergency ... *Oh, Harvey, is it my mother?*”

Unidentified Very Insistent Caller: “Look, lady, Harvey is

a seven-foot rabbit and your mother is irrelevant! This is the president of the US of A and I need the Girl Scouts. The Country needs the Girl Scouts. It's a matter of urgent national security ...."

SCG: "Look, whoever you are, I know the president of the United States of America has better things to do than place prank phone calls to the Girl Scouts! This phone call costs our organization dearly and ..."

UVIC: "What do I need to do, Lady, to convince you that this isn't Harvey, that seven-foot rabbit, and I ain't no Jimmy Steward!"

SCG: "Stewart."

UVIC: "Excuse me?"

SCG: "You meant to say, Jimmy Stewart, the star of that 1950 film about an imaginary rabbit. You said 'Steward,' but the correct name is Stewart."

UVIC: "Well, lady, you take the cake. You got the president's goat talking about a rabbit."

SCG: "The president has a goat? And I started that goat talking about a rabbit?"

UVIC: "Lady, you got ME, the president of the US of A, talking about livestock when I'm calling you about an urgent matter of national security which only YOU and the Girl Scouts are in a position to solve. You ..."

SCG: "You're not kidding, are you? This is actually the voice of the president!"

UVIC: "You got it, Lady. Or at least, you're getting it. Look, I got a real problem here, George W. Bush, may God bless his pea-brain, got this US of A into a financial quagmire by simultaneously starting two fool's errands of wars and creating the biggest bureaucracy of do-nothings since the phone company!"

SCG: "What does this have to do with the Girl Scouts? I don't see how I can help you undo what 'W' hath quagmired."

UVIC: "Yeah, it make take a few generations to pay off all the medical bills from those two wars, but at least we can get rid of that boondoggle called 'Homeland Security' that George created. I know he felt a need to get the country working again, but even the Blue Suits could have thought of a better make-work program than ..."

SCG: "Just how can the Girl Scouts help their country, Mr. President? We are very patriotic, but I just don't see how ..."

UVIC: "You can replace Homeland Security. It's simple really–replace all those fat, middle-aged guys who enjoy harassing the flying public. Replace them with your sweet, young, Girl Scouts. Everybody loves little girls, so the nation's blood pressure will be reduced. And the Green Dresses can sell cookies to the flying public, thereby increasing your cookie revenue exponentially. It's a win-win! What d'ya say?"

SCG: "... Ah ... Let me ... see if I ... have this right. You, Mr. President, want to nationalize the Girl Scouts? You want my girls–my little darlings–to replace the Transportation Safety Administration? I thought you were a free market kind of guy?

UVIC: "Markets, schmarkets! I want to do a deal! Hell, my daddy taught me to make deals and I'm making you a big, big deal! You stand to become, not only the Supremest Cookie Goddess of all freakin' time but to lead the Girl Scouts into a whole new direction. You will be cast in bronze! The Girl Scouts will be providing their country a service while driving cookie income to unforeseen heights. I'm telling you, it's a win-win!"

SCG: "Mr. President, I will take your proposal before the Council of Large Pinafores and see what the ladies say."

UVIC: "Council, smuckshul! My people say those Large Pinafores rubber stamp whatever you put before them. Let's do this deal today and be done with it. I've got nineteen top security office complexes around Washington, D.C., that I can put on the market tomorrow if you give me the green light. Selling them will retire one percent of Dubya's war debts and send a message to our NATO Allies that we don't mess around when it comes to financial responsibility!"

SCG: "I'll tell you what, Mr. President, throw in the

largest of those top security office complexes so I can tell the Pinafores that I've wrangled the D.C. headquarters they've always wanted, and you've got a deal."

UVIC: "Madam Supreme, you've got yourself a deal. I'll even throw in an F-35 to replace that old Lear Jet you're riding in right now. It's due for replacement, so the boys at FAA tell me, and we can retrofit one of our extra F-35s with a cabin by Chris Craft, the luxury boat people. What d'ya say?"

SCG: "I appreciate the thought, Mr. President, but I'd much rather have the Washington Monument. It will make a strong base for the forthcoming Green Dress Broadcasting Network. We're gonna give Martha Stewart a run for her rolling pin!"

UVIC: "My dear, you've got it. My stenographer, Ms. Shiniethighs, is typing out an email to the National Park Service as we speak. The paperwork will be on your desk when you return from Seattle."

VII PRESIDENT TRUMP AUCTIONS OFF THE SMITHSONIAN

NATIONAL MALL, WASHINGTON, D.C.

President Trump, ever a man of action, began to lose interest in his job after nationalizing the Girl Scouts. Selling off eighteen of the now-defunct Department of Homeland Security's nineteen Washington, D.C.-area top secret office complexes had actually retired one point six percent of Dubya's Unnecessary War Debt. Signing the Washington Monument over to the Girl Scouts turned out to be a brilliant move—a transaction estimated by the General Services Administration to save the American people twenty billion dollars a year. President Trump was happier than he had been since running the Univision newsman out of his campaign press conference. After the nationalization of the Girl Scouts, sales of the Department of Homeland Security assets, and privatization of the Washington Monument, a sense of ennui settled over the West Wing.

A Friday-afternoon conversation with Chief of Staff Limbaugh and Press Secretary Coulter was the catalyst for personal revelation. The president had never allowed an intervention, not even when the media reacted—over-reacted, he would say—to the idea of dating his own daughter. What was that all about anyway? The girl was obviously beautiful. Her gene pool could not be questioned. His taste was impeccable. What's to criticize? Okay, maybe she was over-educated, but that was her mother's fault. He'd never required his children to over-indulge in book-learning. Besides that one fault, she was a Regular American Princess. What's not to like?!

Meanwhile, back to the Friday afternoon visit in the Oval Office ... "Limberger," asked Coulter without realizing her faux pas, "What epochal undertaking would re-ignite the president's interest in his work?"

"Harrumph," began Limbaugh, fingering the four

250-count bottles of Viagra in his suit coat pocket, "In my humble opinion, the president has made more out of his first one-hundred days than any of his recent predecessors. He can rest on his laurels, take a couple of weeks at Camp Trump, to recuperate, golf, and leave the running of the Free World to me. His legacy is secure; he can recharge."

"That's just it," retorted Coulter, "his malaise is precisely *that he is restless.* One cannot rest when one is restless. It is a physiological impossibility."

"You're just thinking of Hiroshima," said Limbaugh hautily, "That dog's gentle nature colors your perception of every personality in your life."

"Leave Hiroshima and Nagasaki out of this," Coulter replied, tossing her golden coiffure as she looked away from the impertinent former Broadcasting Prejudices radio host. "The president's mood is affecting his work. Why, just yesterday, he completely missed a discreet opportunity to hit on that young congresswoman from Oklahoma, that blonde with the big ... ah, that precious Republican Blonde. I was just flabbergasted."

The two trusted presidential aides had been discussing President Trump as if he was not sitting across the room from them, jack knife in hand, carving his initials into the Lincoln Desk. At the mention of the leggy congresswoman from Oklahoma–just his type, he had to admit, not one of those Native American darkies–his head lifted from his carving. "Too many congresswomen spoil the hot tub," said the president.

Limbaugh and Coulter exchanged glances. What did the president mean? How could one complain about too many White Republican Goddesses? There was no conceivable reply.

"Maybe a junket," suggested Coulter. "A change of venue might do the president good–revive his spirits."

Since the president didn't bite, Limbaugh jumped into the vacuum. "I hear Thailand is pleasant this time of year. Maybe a foreign policy junket to Southeast Asia would burnish the president's diplomatic credentials while giving his spirits a boost."

"Thing is," offered the president, blowing shavings from his work area, "I've had enough travel this year. What can you come up with right here in my new hometown?" In his mind, the president was trying to hum the tune of *New York, New York*, that old Sinatra number, while thinking of his favorite D.C. spots. It just wasn't working.

Limbaugh's ears perked up. He and Coulter exchanged excited glances. They had engaged the sleeping beast!

"D.C. delights," Coulter thought aloud. "You like Rock Creek Parkway, Mr. President; perhaps you could hold a press conference and rename it for one of your heroes. Say your father ... or Sylvester Stallone?"

"Benito Mussolini," offered the president, who was now admiring his handiwork, a wan smile crossing his face as if comparing this new carving with prior work in the same genre.

"Mussolini may not cast just the desired image," offered Coulter in a tentative tenor.

"Yup, Mussolini it is. Did you know *Il Duche* was my

Uncle Dominic's third cousin, by marriage?"

To say that Limbaugh and Coulter exchanged conspiratorial glances at this point would be like saying that the architect of the Golden Gate Bridge enjoyed his toy blocks as a toddler. At that moment, an inspiration arose between them for which the pride of conception would forever be disputed.

"I thought of it first," Limbaugh would insist in retrospect.

"In your wet dreams," Coulter would counter. "You couldn't sniff out a genius idea like that over your own stink, Limberger!" Coulter could be very caustic, even in her presidentially-dictated tenor. Underneath it all, she hadn't changed all that much.

"If you came up with it," Limbaugh would counter, "Hiroshima must have dropped the bombshell [he was referring to the idea, not the A-bomb] on your brain." They faced facts: the argument was just going to go downhill from there.

What was said–it was unclear just who said it–was, "The

Smithsonian. The Smithsonian Castle and all of her puppies: The American Museum of This History and That. It's the perfect focus for your next project, Mr. President." Once the genius was out of the bottle, so to speak, there was no denying its merit. Any genie in the storm!

A crooked smile spread across the presidential visage. All would soon be well in his world. "An auction," said the president, coming out of his stupor. "We can reduce the federal debt in a *big* way if we auction off all of that old stuff in the Smithsonian. What d'you think, Limbaugh? Can we pay off half of the Federal debt with a month's worth of auction income?"

Limbaugh allowed as how the Treasury could at least wipe out the trillions that future generations now owed on George W's two wars. "Hell, we can probably even afford to give veterans the same medical benefits that congressmen enjoy," Limbaugh gushed before considering how distasteful such an egalitarian policy might sound to his surly boss. It was an ill-considered comment in the office of a Red States president, but it was at least well-intended.

Across the room, President Trump was rising from his desk to gaze out across the South Lawn. Lost in a reverie, the president imagined a Second Statue of Liberty. The new statue he envisioned would stand where the national Christmas tree now stood. It would be fifty feet taller than the illuminated tree, and it would be made of the finest Italian marble. It would be the figure of a man, a self-made man (ignoring, for the sake of argument, that hundred million dollar stake from Daddy). Yes, it would be the Liberty by Trump Monument, the District of Columbia's new crowning jewel and tourist attraction. Illuminated from every angle, it would be a monument for the ages. Inspiring to peoples both domestic and foreign, it would be the highest use of Carrara marble since Michaelangelo knocked out that number of the seated lady holding her slacker son.

There would be plenty of money left over to begin a new collection of knick knacks in each of the Smithsonian museums. Get our artist-friends to donate some new paintings; Grandma Moses must have a granddaughter turning out canvasses right and left nowadays! Maybe get Boeing and Space-X to fill the emptied Air and Space Museum with prototypes for an annual advertising fee–genius! The 4-H Clubs of American would be overjoyed to fill one massive museum with shelves of canned peaches, paintings of bovines, and maybe even a taxidermied Cornish Rock Hen or Billy Goat Gruff. Hell, those Hollywood types would be all over themselves erecting sets from blockbuster movies in the emptied American Museum of Art. It was brilliant. All the world would know it was his idea! Trump could feel it in his bones: auctioning off the contents of the Smithsonian Institution would be his finest hour. He would lean across the walnut podium, shake his gavel at the fat cats drooling over a Hope Diamond, a Frederick Remington bronze, or a Spirit of Saint Louis. He would make them pay! Oh, he would make those fat cats and their lovelies pay! President Trump considered what Federal debts his Auction of the Century could eliminate: Ten years' worth of clandestine war-making in the Middle East! All of those Texas-based contractors who were sent to Louisiana to rebuild stuff after Hurricane Katrina—eighty-six billion dollars spent almost entirely in W's home state. Also, those bombers that Dick Cheney had to have (which are now mothballed on a Wyoming sandlot)! Trump could *just see* the photos that would fill his presidential library: Trump the Master Emptier of Museums! What better way to sell himself to posterity as a Man of the People?

VIII PRESIDENT TRUMP SELLS THE VETERANS ADMINISTRATION

BETHESDA NAVAL HOSPITAL
BETHESDA, MARYLAND

Selling off the contents of the Smithsonian Institution was a large undertaking, even for a Trump. But, as the president himself said when the last of the First Ladies' gowns went to a debutante from Buffalo, "Where there is no vision, the Pope's in the parish." The Secretary of Native Gaslands and Coalfields was saying something about people perishing on the Titanic, which the president felt was inappropriate at a media event of this magnitude. However, the president–who just yesterday had decided not to fire any cabinet member this week—felt that Mr. Cruz deserved a ninety-third chance, so he overlooked the blunder.

Cameras were focused on the small group around the president. Secretary of War, W.A.R. Bombshell, who the president felt was attired inappropriately for such a momentous occasion, was at the podium. Bombshell was discussing her proposal to dig up the Pacific atoll on which the first A-bomb had been tested and ship it to Washington, D.C. She planned to erect it as a protective barrier around the White House. Within the atoll, which Secretary Bombshell proposed to suspend fifty feet above ground level, would be a series of anti-aircraft emplacements designed to protect He Who Fires from being fired upon by any foreign power or over-zealous postal worker equipped with an ultralight helicopter. "Besides," Secretary Bombshell, was saying—lurching forward and back on her spike heels—"The visual effect of a suspended atoll will grant to our president the magnificent halo that he so deserves, so long as his hair does not become entangled in it."

Did she actually say that? The president reconsidered his no-firing-this-week policy. Secretary of Native Gaslands and Coalfields Cruz was thinking that his cabinet seat was safe for at least another week. At the podium, W.A.R. Bombshell was thinking that inserting her personal agenda in today's program might not have come across with the gravitas with which she had so hoped to launch it. *Self-immolation* was the phrase that suddenly came to mind.

The president, suddenly aware that only his decisive action could save the moment, rose from his folding chair, adjusted his ball cap, and strode to the podium, applauding for no reason other than to save Ms. Bombshell from another unfortunate utterance. Blessedly, his deflection worked. All of the assembled military brass began to applaud, and the assembled legion of Paid Applauders (flown in for this occasion from the studio of *The Price is Reasonable*) followed suit.

President He Who Fires took hold of the podium and assessed the situation: the beauty of the cloudless autumn day, the assembled military brass, the paid applauders, and the U.S. Navy Surgeons from Bethesda Naval Hospital. Each surgeon was accompanied by a bevy of lean, blonde nurses. He Who Fires decided that each doctor, in his starched, white lab coat, looked like a carnation surrounded by roses. The nurses were the roses. The roses were more attractive than the carnations, that was evident. *Roses,* thought the president, *come in all colors. Some are genetically blessed with ruby cheeks. Some looked suspiciously Mexican–still, they were nicely rouged and eye-lined. Roses ...*

Abruptly realizing that the microphones were waiting for him to speak, President Trump shook off his reverie, which although enjoyable, was not the point of his appearance here in Bethesda today. Today, He Who Fires remembered, was a really big day. Today, he ... *He* ... the only one capable of making such an amazing deal, was here to announce the merger of the Veterans Administration with Dreamlike, the movie theater chain. Dreamlike's CEO was seated next to the folding chair He Who Fires had just vacated when the president had risen to save Secretary W.A.R. Bombshell from her failing act ... that is ... speech. *Speak*, the president's nerve center insisted, and speak he did:

> My Dear Vice President Payless ... er, Paydown ... er, Palin, Madam Secretary, Generals, Doctors, and Lovelies ... er ... Nurses ... of the esteemed Bethesda Naval Hospital: Your rich tradition of care to our military heroes has served our country long and well. You have cared for our veterans of the War of 1218.

A murmur spread throughout the crowd and smiles seemed more forced than usual as the president continued.

> Your ministrations have gone unsung by all but Francis Scott Offkey, Tiny Tim, and that great cheerleader for your institution, our own W.A.R. Bombshell!

An APPLAUSE! light flashed out of sight of the TV cameras. Paid Applauders did their thing.)

> Your forebears worked day and night to create piles of sawed-off limbs during our heroic

> Civil War–legs, arms, appendages which today could be saved with modern ...

The president was rudely interrupted by the U.S. Naval Academy Band, which–frustrated with the president's abrupt assumption of the podium–decided to play *Hail to the Chief* right in the middle of his speech! The brass section blocked out all other sounds. Only ... the tune came out as *Hair to the Chief!* Upon closer inspection, He Who Fires realized that the high school band from Ferguson, Missouri, had tricked him by absconding with the uniforms of the U.S. Naval Academy Band! How had they been admitted to the hospital grounds? Had they also stolen the Naval Academy bus? If so, who was the complicit bus driver who'd cooperated in their sneaky ploy? Adjusting the bill of his ball cap, the president remembered his motto emblazoned thereon, "Make America White Male Again!" *Surely*, he thought, *hospital security must have realized that a busload of Americans of Another Color could not have been the actual U.S. Naval Academy Band!*

Why is everyone laughing? He Who Fires realized that the admirals and generals were laughing. *Laughing!* The president heard the Paid Applauders laughing. He recognized Miss Coulter's tenor laughter, then he realized that the cameramen were guffawing. Remembering his late father's admonitions, He Who Fires mused, *When something works, and it's not clear whose idea it was, just let folks assume it was yours!* Leaving the podium for the moment, President Trump beamed his best Teddy Roosevelt grin—all teeth, ear to ear—and strolled across the stage. Finding himself captivated by the catchy rhythm, he skipped, then swirled, as if doing a waltz solo before the TV cameras. *Putin may bear his old-man chest on horseback,* the president thought, *but can he swing like me?* It was a news cycle bonanza!

Decorum was regained after the band—following up *Hair to the Chief* with a medley of *Some Enchanted Hospital Closing, Smoke Gets Up My Nose,* and Vice President Palin's personal favorite, *On A Clear Day You Can See Vladivostok.* Timing being everything, President Trump just laid it on the line. "In one of the biggest deals of my presidency, I have sold the Veterans Administration. Well, actually, I didn't really sell it, but I did merge it. We found the best M&A opportunity in today's market, and we merged it right out of the government!" Now He Who Fires was feeling his second wind. "We have merged the V.A., an organization badly in need of modernization, woefully lacking in Big Data knowhow, and technologically challenged, with that industry-leading powerhouse, Dreamlike Cinemas Worldwide. Yes, we have found a partner that understands big, empty buildings where people sit for hours. Our partner understands food service, patron in-flow, and out-flow. They have those vehicles that clean up an entire parking lot overnight, removing discarded pennies, popcorn boxes, plastic straws, and bird poop without a trace!"

"But Mr. President, how can a movie theater chain serve the growing needs of veterans?" A rumpled NPR reporter blurted the question that was on everyone's mind.

"Scalability," replied the president. "Dreamlike understands the scale on which today's veterans deserve to be moved in and then out. Besides, who but Dreamlike deals with carpet cleaning on the scale of the Veterans Administration? No more tile floors for our veterans! We are giving them the very best in their waiting rooms, colonoscopy suites, hemorrhoid centers, and post-surgical facilities," intoned the president, his good cheer returned and his ball cap pulled low to allow the cameras to catch its glittery stitching.

"Dreamlike already has facilities with lots of parking in communities presently unserved by the V.A. Think of the driving time it will save our heroic veterans. And every waiting room will be fitted with a Dreamlike screen! The opportunities to reduce payrolls will enhance patient treatment time while combining popcorn preparation and urine testing staffs for greater employee satisfaction! It is a win-win deal and ..."

Dreamlike's CEO had been prepared to follow up the president's announcement with a talk of his own, but discretion being the better part of colonoscopy, he kept the speech neatly folded in his jacket pocket. He departed the dais along with Vice President Palin, who was mumbling about getting Tom Hanks on board as a national security advisor, given his military service in *Forrest Gump* and his legal training for *Bridge of Spies*. "Actually," the vice president continued, "if you should decide to do a re-make with a small title change, I might be interested in the title role for *Bridget of Spies*." The Dreamlike CEO was saved from responding by a news team urgently requesting an interview.

IX PRESIDENT TRUMP SELLS CALIFORNIA

LAS VEGAS CONVENTION CENTER
LAS VEGAS, NEVADA

Woody Guthrie's ballad, *This Land is Your Land*, was blaring from the sound system as President Trump made his way through a raucous crowd. Placards bobbed above heads, most of which were wearing ball caps emblazoned with the president's motto, "Make America White Male Again." The heat of broadcast camera lights could be felt on the stage, where Press Secretary Coulter was tapping the microphone and enunciating clearly, "The president is in the building," in her trademark tenor.

From the side of the hall where the president had not yet been sighted, cheers greeted Coulter's announcement.

Eight synchronized barbershop quartets broke out in song to the tune of *Oh! Susanna:*

Yo, Montana, won't ya' sit up an' see,
The president's in the building just talkin' to you and me!
Watch Golden-haired Trump kick some butt
In pursuit of our li-burr-tee!

Meanwhile, President Trump was making his way through the crowd, glad-handing representatives of chambers of commerce, realty companies, drug store chains, and auto dealership consortiums. A lobbyist from the aerospace giant, Boeing, shadowed the Secret Service detail, his grey suit and yellow silk tie standing out against their red, white, and blue uniforms, his bald head distinctive among their red fezes.

The strains of barbershop quartet lyrics were reverberating from every corner of the large hall, adding to the president's own spirits as he took the podium, his ball cap raised at arms-length. From the floor, sounds of folding chairs gnashing mingled with cheering and applause. Grasping the podium as if it were a yard-long Philly cheese-steak sandwich, President Trump began to address the throng.

"The administration is taking the initiative once again! Today–by executive order–I have taken a huge step toward *making America white male again*," this last phrase almost shouted, as the president emphasized his campaign motto. Responding to He Who Fires, the crowd lurched to its feet row by row, as if choreographed, creating a wave of visual as well as audible applause from the first row to the last. "We have taken a step toward higher quality of life for all of white male America!" This time the wave reversed, beginning with the furthest row and cresting forward until it seemed to lap upon the base of the podium like an Atlantic breaker.

From the section reserved for patriotic survivalists at the extreme right side of the audience, a cacophonous cheer–assault rifles firing blanks–placed a staccato emphasis on the applause. President Trump, returning his ball cap to his head, nodded appreciatively to the survivalists. A CBS-TV cameraman tripped over a reporter from *Paris*

Match, causing a momentary commotion (and resulting in a presidential press corps romance that would later be compared to the Matalin-Carville marriage).

The next words from the president's mouth silenced the entire room. "Today, we have sold California." Not quite sure how to react to the president's latest deal, the ball-capped crowd sat, silent ... and stunned.

It took a minute for the upside of the president's latest deal to sink in. As this happened, attendees began to respond by lifting their ball caps to salute the president. This was beyond their wildest imaginings. This was ... big!

"California no longer looks like Amurica, so we've sold that real estate to land-hungry Taiwan. Taiwan has agreed to pay for the real estate by paying off the remainder of the federal debt in 72 installments. Ford Motor Credit is handling the transaction since it is too big for any of my friends on Wall Street. We are now a debt-free country, from sea to Taiwanese Sea!

"The generous chambers of commerce of Oregon and

Washington have agreed to become the new San Francisco and Los Angeles, respectively, and San Diego has agreed to move to the Mississippi Gulf Shore. The resulting transaction will *make Amurica eleven percent more white male!*"

At the allusion to the familiar campaign slogan, the audience seemed to catch its breath. A cheer arose, but it was less than what could be characterized a Texas-sized cheer. However, the delegations from the states of Washington, Oregon, Nevada, and Arizona make their huzzahs heard and boosted the president's morale. He knew in his heart that he had done the right thing, getting the country out of debt and making it more white male again. As Faux News would later editorialize, the president "had the courage of his baseball caps."

Washington think tanks were abuzz with opinions, concerns, potential collateral disruptions to the economy, to the body politic, and to the country's social fabric. Would the re-made geography of the country result in faster economic growth? How much of the movie industry would move to the new Los Angeles, now that it would be Seattle's sister city? How would the loss of California's Central Valley impact American grocery prices–possibly even eating habits? Would blueberries become the new strawberries? Would almond orchards suddenly spring up in New Mexico? What about Paso Robles Vintners–how could they relocate? Perhaps Americans would find themselves savoring Taiwan wine from Sonoma County?

In Findlay, Ohio, "Flag City, USA," speculation surrounded the removal of one star from the national flag. Faux News was first on the scene, interviewing stalwarts of the local posts of veterans organizations. Which star should be removed? Might the "California Star" remain on the flag, but be shown in black for mourning? Or might that star perhaps be rendered in green to signify the end of the federal debt? Would the revision of the flag be minimalist–retaining the blue field for stars? Or if a macro approach were adopted, might the stars now become blue and be sprinkled across the thirteen stripes willy-nilly?

Of course, the most consequential conversations were going on in Silicon Valley. Go Taiwan or stay USA? That was the question. If moving the Tech industry *en masse,* might Boulder, Colorado, seem the logical relocation site. Yoga was already practiced at the Boulder Public Library on Arapahoe Street every morning. However, moving the headquarters of Apple, Google, Yahoo!, Oracle, Tesla, and Facebook–plus a thousand other tech firms–could prove a challenge in a state whose current highest-ranked location on Google Maps was Whatever, USA. Larry Page and Tim Cook agreed that they were just not "Whatever" kind of guys. Their workers worried about housing in a state not known for its forest industries. Assurances were forthcoming from the long haul team at J.B. Hunt Truck Lines in Lowell, Arkansas, who placed one hundred eighty-seven new Freightliner rigs on order just to satisfy anticipated demand due to the sale of California. J.B. Hunt expedited a sales team to San Francisco and Cupertino with the message that no long-haul job was too big for them.

Detroit made a play to become the new Silicon Valley. The Motor City surprised critics with its offer to make fourteen million square feet of former auto-manufacturing space available free to tech firms, provided that the companies assure Detroit of three million new housing units within four years. Sergio Page liked the idea. "Detroit's climate is ideal for server farms," he was reported as saying to an anxious reporter from the *Detroit Free Press.*

Michigan Public Radio was the first to report Mark Zuckerberg's demand that the Detroit Institute of Arts acquire the collection of San Francisco's M. H. de Young Memorial Museum before he would consider making the move. Steve Jobs' widow, Laurene Powell Jobs, broke her media silence to insist that the Asian Art Museum of San Francisco also be relocated if she and her book club were to find Detroit an acceptable cultural community. Ms. Jobs' demand was met coolly by directors at the Detroit Institute of Art, which cited its rare Korean Head of Buddha. Just a hundred and thirty miles to the east of Detroit, the Cleveland Institute of Art called a press conference in the office of its director and spent twenty-seven minutes of CNN primetime touting its collection of Japanese and Korean art as "world-class." A Detroit young artists group weighed in with a sculpture show announcement, featuring the work of sixteen young Asian-American artists. Among the sculptures to be displayed, they announced, would be a ten-ton stainless steel homage to Hiroshima by a Japanese-born, University of Michigan-educated rising star recently profiled in *Artists of the Foreseeable Future* magazine.

In Congress, the House of Representatives considered the design of the flag its primary issue for the coming session. Senators had to deal with the delicate matters of the deal with Taiwan, but Representatives in the House were focused on the symbolism of the deal. "Social Security recipients better get their act together," said the Red Suit leader. "The national belt will have to be tightened, and our seniors need to lead by example. No whining when deals are hot and President Trump has proven to be the hottest dealer since ... since ... since President Coolidge bought the Niagara Falls!"

Someone in the cheap seats of the Red Suit section whispered, "President Coolidge didn't buy Niagara Falls, they were part of New York State since Aaron Burr and Jefferson Davis had that duel ...."

Meanwhile, gasoline was scarce in Southern California, as convoys of semis headed east loaded with movie sets, computer farms, Pecan tree seedlings, and other undisclosed agricultural cuttings. Interstate 80 between Auburn and Blue Canyon was backed up approaching the mountains. The secretary of National Gaslands and Coalfields called on the Coast Guard to helicopter fuel to stranded truckers and motorists. Secretary Cruz's order was a breach of cabinet etiquette which angered Secretary of War W.A.R. Bombshell. Her diamond choker exploded all over the oval office when Limbaugh mentioned the plan, unaware that Cruz had not cleared it with her previously.

In the executive suite of the Getty Center, weighty matters were under discussion, namely the fate of two magnificent collections of art in Los Angeles County. The Italianate villa nestled into an oceanfront ravine, a work of art in itself, could obviously not be moved. Might the Taiwanese government consider allowing the Getty organization to continue to manage that site as an international cultural exchange of some sort? It remained to be seen, and diplomacy was fluid.

Many were adamant that relocation to another state was the only acceptable option. Omaha, Nebraska, was the board's venue of choice for the hilltop collection. It's home of massive stone construction would also have to be abandoned, but its paintings, sculptures, and artifacts–if carefully packaged–could certainly be transported halfway across the continent. Curators were concerned about the effects of humidity on paintings and textile art during the journey. A team of art movers the size of a small expeditionary force would be required to handle planning, crating, and transporting the 122,026 pieces of art in the museum's inventory. Warren Buffet and his people were quick to offer a new home for the Getty collection in the Omaha area. An international search was already underway to secure the services of an elite architectural firm with experience in world-class museum design.

The Los Angeles Symphony Orchestra was in talks with Halliburton on plans to disassemble the Disney Concert Hall, sheet by stainless steel sheet, and reassemble it at a new location. Dick Cheney, whom Halliburton brought out of retirement to manage the project, was quoted as saying that Seattle, Minneapolis, and Washington, D.C., were bidding for rights to rebuild the Frank Gehry structure and host the symphony company. Fearful for their jobs, members of the Seattle Symphony's percussion section announced a Tympani-In, the first every announced, according to *Modern Symphony* magazine. The report said a Tympani-In was a kind of auditory hunger strike in which musicians drummed without ceasing until their concerns were addressed. Whether or not drummers actually took nourishment during the Tympani-In was in dispute at publication time.

At the waterfront in Long Beach, the negotiations that

were underway to find a suitable new home for RMS Queen Mary presented more challenges than first anticipated. While the arrival of the Queen Mary was guaranteed to spike interest in the hospitality industry wherever she might go, her size and the expense of towing her through the Panama Canal would prove costly to any prospective host. Furthermore, construction of adequate docking facilities would challenge any municipal budget.

Tampa was interested but declined when it was determined that the Queen Mary's plumbing system was incompatible with that of the city waterfront. Baltimore backed out when city officials agreed that a substantial black and white monument on the waterfront would only draw unwanted atttention to the city's racial woes. Portsmouth, Maine, put forward a surprisingly strong bid, only to retract the offer when the region's French-American community fussed uncharitably about the use of tax funds to accommodate a British vessel, even if tourism might spike as a result.

In the end, RMS Queen Mary found a berth created just

for her below the bluffs of Martha's Vineyard. Marketing surveys showed conclusively that the summer vacationers who frequented the Vineyard were favorably disposed to spending even more of their disposable income aboard the great ship, if located near their favorite East Coast vacation spot. The CBS *Sixty Minutes* marketing team offered a seven-figure budget to move the Queen Mary to Martha's Vinyard in honor of the late TV essayist, Andy Rooney, provided that the premiere restaurant aboard the ship would be renamed "Eyebrows" in his honor.

In a related development, The Museum of Modern Art in New York City announced an agreement with the Queen Mary's owners to establish a branch museum inside the unused boilers of the great ship. Works of metal art by union pipefitters were rumored to dominate the first exhibition once the new museum was open to the public, a date as yet uncertain.

Meanwhile, in the White House, President Trump was said to be suffering a second—and much more accute—case of ennui. While the James Brady Press Room continued to host frequent press briefings by Ms. Coulter, fascination with her now-familiar tenor had fallen off and attendance was flagging. Commenting on the trend, *Business Week* editors were overheard at the water cooler griping that the president's absence from media events might contribute to the economic downturn that had begun by the sale of California. "When you sell off a state with an economy the size of Sweden's, there's bound to be repercussions," one was reported to have whispered rather dramatically.

On any given evening, limousines loaded with leggy blondes were reported entering the White House grounds in rapid succession. Loud party-like noises could be heard emanating from the White House bowling alley at all hours of the night, according to the *National Enquirer*. Each Thursday morning, Dr. Phil's personal limo was observed approaching 1600 Pennsylvania Avenue at precisely 8:54 a.m. President Trump had not been seen in public for eight weeks.

The newly-named Surgeon General, Dr. Carson,

was mum. Leaked reports indicated that a regimen of pyramid rice puree had been initiated. At Republican headquarters, there were audible exhales of relief at the latest rumor. The ultimate cure, it was rumored–the so-called Big Bang Treatment–was being withheld as a last resort. The party chairman, Mr. Plastic, sent the president an urgent message of cheer:

THE REPUBLICAN NATIONAL COMMITTEE

AND IT'S SEE-THROUGH CHAIRMAN,

MR. PLASTIC,

ARE PLEASED TO ANNOUNCE THAT

HENCEFORTH, LINCOLN-DAY DINNERS

SHALL BE CELEBRATED AS

LINCOLN-NIXON-TRUMP DAY

DINNERS, IN HONOR OF OUR GREATEST

LEADERS AND PHILOSOPHICAL IDOLS!

If Mr. Plastic's gesture of cheer had the desired effect on the president, it was not noted in any media. Limousines of leggy blondes continued to come and go. Dr. Phil's limousine continued to come and go. The stock market continued to decline.

Trump hotels and casinos advertised deals in TV spots featuring shouting blondes. At 90 decibels, the bikini-clad beauties offered "deals that will make your neighbors jealous! *Really seriously jealous!* We're not talking new-lawn-mower-envy here; we mean *jealous!*"

Advertising Age speculated about the identity of the copywriter for those ads. "Even the Eye-ah-tollah himself gets better ratings than the new Trump Hotels spots," one *Ad Age* executive was reported as commenting over his three-martini lunch at a certain Italian restaurant on Madison Avenue. The Bully Pulpit was growing cobwebs. The White House website went down for thirty-six hours. The situation only came to light when a sixth-grade student from Hartford, Connecticut, complained that she could not complete her social studies homework. Marine Corps

One received unnecessary oil changes. Aboard Air Force One, bored security guards challenged under-employed Secret Service agents to a night of continuous poker. Nobody won.

At the National Cathedral, a National Good Spirits Seminar was being held. Clerics from thirty-nine denominations arrived from across the country. The joke on the street was that it was actually a "National Bad Spirits" event. The sale of California–while it had eliminated the federal debt–had lead to a deflation of everyone's spirits. What with the American flag now sporting a black star–which Senator Cory Booker was quick to dub "America's black eye"–and the president unseen for weeks, the national mood was worse than gloomy.

In Boston, taxi drivers stopped singing arias. One ABC News commentator, attempting humor, reported on-air that "the slump in the national mood was now Verdi-fiable." In Chicago, the satirical newspaper, *The Onion*, threatened to change its name to *The Turnip* if the national mood did not rebound. Circulation at *The Onion* was reported to be in the compost heap.

The Audit Bureau of Circulation, which tracks readership of periodicals, reported that newsstand sales of all magazines were declining with every issue. The Neilson organization, tracking America's TV viewing habits, confirmed that only one broadcast company seemed to be prospering in the post-California sale economy. It was Faux News. A Harvard professor of media studies, commenting on the singular prosperity of Faux News during the slump, was quoted as saying, "Misery loves company, and in this case, the company loves misery."

A New York City doorman who was holding the door of a limo when he heard it, leaked this from the new head of Faux News: "Mike Huckabee couldn't sell salvation to a bum in this economy–even if he threw in a month of meat-and-threes in the Imperial Suite!"

The news executive later recanted the comment, saying in part, "I have it on good authority that even Barry Goldwater's return from the dead could not wake up this White

House."

Over at the Federal Reserve Bank, executives were huddled in Janet Yellen's office. Usually a talkative group, the suits were glum. Someone from the Second District suggested first-ever negative interest rates.

"Pay people to borrow money!?" asked Yellen, undone by the temerity of the suggestion (though privately, she considered it innovative, even sensible). "People are happy that the president sold California, aren't they? Unemployment is under three percent, what with all the relocation work and the replacement housing boom. What does it take to satisfy people?"

Just then, an aide rushed in holding a piece of paper that turned out to be a screen-shot of a breaking news story. Yellen grasped the sheet from the young woman's shaking hand and read aloud:

Emirate Said to Offer Trump
999 Trillion for the USA

[Dubai, UAE] According to reliable sources,

the Emirate of Dubai has made an offer of US$999T to purchase the United States of America, a report that our mole at the White House says is being taken seriously. The mole, speaking on condition of anonymity, reported that the president is tempted "because he has never made a deal that big."

The End

BIOGRAPHICAL NOTE

Duke Wallace writes in that time-honored tradition of political satirists that reaches as far back in American history as the Revolutionary War period. Tom Paine, Ben Franklin, and their contemporaries used creatively-signed epistles to stir sentiment in favor of home rule. Wallace is both a former Marine and a one-time Republican political operative. Besides, he is a lifelong student of American history. If Mr. Wallace considers the value of his fully-attached neck a higher value than fleeting fame, who are we to cast the first stone?

Just the sort of fellow to be aware that he's inside the caldera of a volcano when visiting Yellowstone National Park, Mr. Wallace lives with his wife and dog in a domicile near the Main Street of a small Midwestern town. Rumors that he and the Mrs. share a weekly canasta evening with the Mittys are unfounded.

SHARE WITH YOUR FRIENDS

To order boatloads of this little book to share with friends, we recommend that you begin with your local bookseller. If your needs cannot be satisfied there, contact

Chicago Distribution Center at:
Phone: 800-621-2736
Email: khyzy@uchicago.edu

Or U.S. mail:
Orders
Chicago Distribution Center
11030 S. Langley
Chicago, IL 60628

When ordering extravagantly, be sure to request the boatload price schedule!